GREAT EXPECTATIONS

by Charles Dickens

Abridged and adapted by T. Ernesto Bethancourt

A PACEMAKER CLASSIC

Fearon Education
Belmont, California

Other Pacemaker Classics

The Adventures of Tom Sawyer
The Deerslayer
Dr. Jekyll and Mr. Hyde
Frankenstein
Jane Eyre
The Jungle Book
The Last of the Mohicans
The Moonstone
Robinson Crusoe
A Tale of Two Cities
The Three Musketeers
The Time Machine
Treasure Island
20,000 Leagues Under the Sea
Two Years Before the Mast

Library of Congress Catalog Card Number: 86-81452

ISBN 0-8224-9260-1

Printed in the United States of America

1. 9 8 7 6 5 4 3

Contents

Introduction

Great Expectations, by Charles Dickens, is one of the most famous novels ever written. Set in 19th-century England, it tells the story of Philip Pirrip, an orphan, who is being raised by his sister and her husband. As a young man, "Pip" learns that an unknown person has set aside a great deal of money for him.

Pip travels to London intending to live life as a gentleman. He eventually learns that his "great expectations" are not anything like he imagined them to be. Pip is forced to reexamine his values and to establish a life that is not based on wealth.

Charles Dickens is recognized as one of the finest writers in history. Born in England in 1812, he spent his early years as a reporter for a London newspaper. He wrote his first novel, *The Pickwick Papers*, in 1836-37. In the following years he wrote such memorable novels as *Nicholas Nickleby*, *David Copperfield*, and *A Tale of Two Cities*.

Many of Dickens's works describe the terrible living and working conditions of the English poor. His stories contain serious criticism of the way many of the unfortunate people in England were being treated. But many of these stories are also filled with humor. *Great Expectations*, written in 1860-61, is considered Dickens's greatest novel.

1 *In the Churchyard*

My family name is Pirrip, and my first name Philip. When I was a baby, the name was too hard for me to say. So, I called myself *Pip*, and came to be called Pip by everybody else.

I never knew my parents. I was raised by my sister, Mrs. Joe Gargery, who was married to the village blacksmith. We lived in the marsh country, down by the river and not far from the sea. All I knew of my father and mother (photographs hadn't been invented yet) were their gravestones in the churchyard. I had discovered this place when I was about six. Since the church was only about a mile from where I lived, I used to go there often.

On the day before Christmas of my seventh year, I found myself again looking at the gravestones. I was trying to imagine what my parents had been like. It was late in the afternoon, and growing dark. The raw wind blowing in from the sea was howling among the gravestones, and it made me shiver. I started to feel sad and lonely, and I began to cry.

"Don't make a sound!" cried a terrible voice, as a man rose up from behind some other gravestones. "Keep still, you little devil, or I'll cut your throat!"

He was a fearful man, all in rough gray clothes. He had a broken chain on his leg. He had no hat, his shoes were broken, and he looked awful. His teeth chattered in the cold air as he grabbed me by the chin.

"Oh! Don't cut my throat, sir," I cried. "Please don't do it!"

"Tell me your name!" said the man. "Quick!"

"Pip, sir."

"Once more," said the man. "I didn't hear you."

"Pip. Pip, sir."

"Show me where you live. Point out the place!"

I pointed to where our town was. The man looked at me for a while. Suddenly, he grabbed my ankles and turned me upside down. He went through my pockets. There was nothing in them but a piece of bread. Then he set me down on a high gravestone. He ate the bread as if he hadn't eaten in ages. Then he turned to me and said, "Now look here. Where's your mother?"

I pointed to her gravestone. "There, sir," I said.

"And that's your father, next to her, eh?" said the man.

"Yes, sir."

"Then who do you live with?" he asked. "That is, if I let you live."

"With my sister, Mrs. Joe Gargery . . . the black-smith's wife," I said.

"A blacksmith, eh?" said the man, looking at the chain on his leg. "Tell me, boy. Do you know what a file is?"

"Yes, sir."

"And you know what food is?"

"Yes, sir."

"You get me a file," he said, picking me up and shaking me. "And get me some food. Or I'll cut out your heart and liver!" He looked around him. "I'm not alone, you know," he said. "There's a young man with me. You don't want to know him. Next to him, I'm an angel. I can't say the awful things he'll do to you, unless you get me what I want."

He made me swear I'd help him. I promised I'd be back, early the next morning. As I ran for home, I kept looking for the terrible other man. I didn't see anyone. I was so scared that I ran all the way home without stopping.

When I got home, my sister wasn't there. I asked Joe, the blacksmith, where she was. "Out looking for you, boy," he told me. "She didn't know what had happened to you. And is she ever mad! She took the Tickler with her."

I ought to explain about the Tickler. It's a long stick that my sister used to beat me with. And she didn't need much reason, either. I guess my sister had a good heart. After all, she raised me when my parents died. As she said, she raised me "by hand." That's not quite true. She really raised me by *stick*.

When my sister, Mrs. Joe, got home, she came after me with the Tickler. Then, as if she were sorry, she gave both me and Joe a slice of bread and butter. I hid mine when no one was looking. I had promised to bring food to the man in the marshes.

Because it was Christmas Eve, I had a lot of work to do. Tomorrow, we would have company for dinner. Mrs. Joe was making special dishes. As I helped Joe get things ready for company, I heard a sound like thunder.

"What was that?" I asked.

"Cannon," said Joe. "It came from the prison ship in the river. A convict must have gotten away. They use cannon as a signal."

"Please, Joe," I asked, "what's a convict?"

"I'll tell you," my sister said. "Men who are killers. Men who steal. They are people who do bad things. And just like you, they're full of questions. Now get to bed!"

She hit me a few times, and I ran for my bed. But I couldn't sleep. At dawn I went downstairs, while everyone was asleep. I took some bread, cheese, and a pie from the kitchen. I also took a bottle of brandy. Then, I got a file from Joe's black-smith shop. Even though I was scared of him, I went off to find "my" convict. For that was what he had to be: a convict from the prison ship!

2 *The Convicts Are Caught*

It was a cold, damp morning. I walked fast to keep warm. In a short time I was at the meeting place. I saw the convict right away. He was sitting with his back to me. I thought it might be nice if I surprised him with breakfast. I came up behind him and tapped him on the shoulder. He jumped to his feet and turned to me. It wasn't the same man!

He was dressed just like "my" convict, except he had a hat. The stranger swore at me and tried to hit me. But he was so weak from being out in the cold that he missed. Then he ran off into the morning fog. I shook all over. He had to be that "other man" my convict spoke of.

I walked on and found my convict. I gave him the food and brandy I'd stolen. He went at the food like a starving man, wolfing his breakfast down. "I'm afraid you're not leaving much for the other fellow," I said.

"What other fellow?" asked the convict.

"The young man you spoke of who was hiding with you."

"Oh, ah!" he said with a laugh. "He doesn't want any food."

"He looked hungry to me," I said.

"Looked? When?"

"Just now."

"Where?"

"Over there," I said, pointing. "He was half-asleep when I found him. I thought he was you." The convict grabbed me. "He was dressed like you," I went on, "but he had a hat."

"Did you notice anything else about him?" asked the man.

"His face was bruised," I said.

"Here?" said the man, touching his left cheek.

"Yes, sir."

"Where is he?" growled the convict. "Let me just get my hands on him! Oh, curse this chain on my leg! Give me that file, boy."

The convict began cutting away at the chain on his leg. I pointed out where the other man had run into the fog. It was getting late in the morning. I knew that my sister and Joe would be up soon. I told the convict I had to go. He didn't seem to notice. So, I just slipped away. The last I saw of him, he was still using the file on the leg chain.

"Where have you been?" said my sister, as soon as I walked in.

"In town, listening to Christmas carols," I lied.

"Get busy around here," she said, "or I'll get after you with the Tickler!" I began to help Joe straighten up the house. Our company was due to arrive soon. Mr. Wopsle, the church clerk, Mr. Hubble, the wheel maker, and his wife, and Joe's uncle, Mr. Pumblechook, were invited.

Mr. Pumblechook always brought the same present each Christmas: two bottles of sherry wine. I sat at the dinner table, listening to the grown-ups talk. I also watched them eat all the best parts of the meal. I got little more than scraps, with gravy on them. And all through the meal, I was scared to death. For as soon as the meal was over, the company would be ready for some pie—the pie I had stolen and given to "my" convict!

At last the meal was over. My sister got up to get the pie for dessert. I couldn't take it anymore. I ran for the door. As I opened the door to run out, I ran right into a party of soldiers, all with guns. One of them had a pair of handcuffs. "Here, you," he said. "Look at these!"

I nearly died. Somehow, they must have found out that I had helped the convict. They had come to take me away! Just then, my sister came into the room. "The pie is gone!" she said. Then she saw the soldiers.

"Excuse me," said the officer in charge, "I am chasing an escaped convict. I need to see the blacksmith."

"What for?" said my sister.

"These handcuffs are broken. If I catch the convict, they won't hold him. Can they be fixed?"

Joe came from the table and looked the handcuffs over. "Yes, I can fix them, but it'll take time. I'll have to start up a fire in my forge."

"Well, let's get to it," said the soldier.

I felt a lot better. The soldiers weren't looking for me, after all. I went with Joe and the soldiers into Joe's shop. Mr. Wopsle and Mr. Pumblechook came, too. Mr. Pumblechook passed around a bottle of wine, while Joe worked on the handcuffs. In a short time, Mr. Pumblechook made friends with the soldiers. Soon, the handcuffs were fixed. The soldiers were getting ready to go.

"Need any help?" Joe asked the officer. "We can come with you."

The officer said it would be all right if they came along. I asked my sister if I could go, too. To my surprise, she said yes. Mr. Pumblechook and Mr. Hubble didn't want to go. But Mr. Wopsle came with us. We went off to the marshes, staying behind the armed men.

We hadn't gone far, when we heard shouting. The soldiers got their guns ready. Then, we found "my" convict. He was in a ditch, fighting with the other convict I'd seen. And did they go at it! The soldiers had to drag them apart.

"Let me at him!" cried my convict. "I was bringing him back to the prison ship!"

The other convict was the man I'd seen early that morning. My convict had found him, all right. The soldiers didn't believe him, at first. Then, my convict explained. "I hate this man more than I hate prison," he told the soldiers. "I don't mind going back, if I know this vile creature goes, too. Look, I could have gotten away, alone. You can see I got the chain off my leg."

"And how did you do that?" asked the soldier. I nearly died inside. Would my convict tell on me? Would the soldiers then take me away, too? Even though it was cold out, I began to sweat.

"I got a file from the blacksmith shop, in town," my convict said. "There was some food, too. I stole a pie and some brandy." As he said these words, he gave me a hard look, as if to say, "Don't worry. I won't tell on you."

And indeed, he did not tell. The soldiers took the two convicts away. But I shall never forget that look I got. With all the excitement over, Joe,

Mr. Wopsle, and I walked back home. Halfway there, I got so tired that Joe carried me the rest of the way. I fell asleep in his arms. It had been quite a Christmas for me!

3 *Miss Havisham and Estella*

In those days, I went to school at Mr. Wopsle's great-aunt's house. Maybe I shouldn't say, "went to school." I was never taught anything much. The old lady used to sleep through the lessons she was supposed to teach. But I tried my best to learn.

It was about a year after "my" convict had been caught, that I wrote my first letter. Not having anyone else to write to, I wrote it to Joe. As I look back, it was terribly done. Hardly anything was spelled right. But I was so proud of myself, I showed it to Joe.

mI deEr JO i opE U r krWitE wEll i opE i shAl soN B HaBell 4 2 teeDge U JO aN theN We shOrl B sO glOdd aN wEn i M preNgtd 2 U JO wOt larX an blEve ME inf xn PiP

Joe looked at the letter. He said it was just fine. "Why, here's a J," said Joe, "and an O, and a J-O. Joe."

"It was then I knew that Joe couldn't read much more than his name. And even that, he spelled wrong. I made up my mind that once I was a good reader, I would teach Joe, too. I knew we would spend a lot of time together. I was going to become Joe's apprentice at the blacksmith's shop. Even if I did spell apprenticed *preNgtd*.

One day, not long after that, my sister came home, very excited. She had been out shopping. Mr. Pumblechook was with her. He had given her some good news. Miss Havisham, one of the richest women in town, had sent him a message. She had a niece who needed someone to play with. And I was to be the lucky playmate! I was to spend the night at Mr. Pumblechook's, and the next morning go to Miss Havisham's big house.

My sister scrubbed me so hard my skin turned red. She had me put on my Sunday church clothes.

My shirt was so stiff I could hardly bend my body. Then Mr. Pumblechook led me outside to his horse and cart. We climbed in and started out for Mr. Pumblechook's house.

The next morning, Mr. Pumblechook took me to Miss Havisham's house. It was an old brick house with many iron bars on it. Mr. Pumblechook and I had to stop at the big iron gate in front of the house. He rang a bell, and a window opened. A clear voice asked, "What name?"

"Pumblechook," cried my guide.

"Quite right," said the voice. The window closed. A young lady came out of the house and opened the gate.

"This is Pip," said Mr. Pumblechook.

"This is Pip, is it?" said the young lady. She was very pretty and seemed very proud. "Come in, Pip."

Mr. Pumblechook was about to come in also, when the girl stopped him with the gate. "Oh," she said, "do you wish to see Miss Havisham?"

"If Miss Havisham wishes to see me," said Mr. Pumblechook.

"Ah," said the girl, "but you see she doesn't."

Even though the girl was very young, about my age, she made Mr. Pumblechook look small and unimportant. He turned red in the face. Then, as if *I* had done it, he told me in a loud voice to watch my manners. Then he left.

The girl led me across the courtyard. Young as she was, she acted like a queen. And she kept calling me "boy," as if I didn't have a real name. We went in through a side door. The whole inside of the house was dark. The girl picked up a lit candle and led me to a room upstairs. She opened the door and said, "Go in."

"After you," I said, trying to show good manners.

"Don't be silly, boy," she said. "I'm not going in." Then she left, taking the candle with her. I stood in darkness, in front of the door. I knocked, and a voice told me to enter.

It was a big room. The light came only from candles. It was ten in the morning, but there was no sunlight in the room, at all. Then I saw her—the strangest lady I had ever seen.

She was sitting in an armchair in the middle of the room. She was dressed in rich clothes—silk, lace, and satin—and all in white. Her shoes were white. She also wore a long white veil and had some wedding flowers in her hair. On a dressing table next to her were some bright jewels. She wasn't finished dressing, I thought. She wore only one white shoe. The other was on the floor, near her chair. Then I looked closer.

Everything white she wore was old—so old that the white had begun to turn yellow. She was like a young bride, grown terribly old. She was thin as a rail, but I guessed she once was heavier. Her dress hung on her in sagging folds.

"Who is it?" she asked.

"Pip, ma'am."

"Pip?"

"Mr. Pumblechook brought me here, ma'am. I have come . . . to play."

"Come nearer. Let me look at you. Come close."

When I was up close, I saw that her watch, which lay on the table, had stopped. It read twenty minutes to nine. A clock in the corner had stopped, too—at the same time.

"Look at me," said Miss Havisham. "Are you afraid of a woman who hasn't seen the sun since you were born?"

"No," I lied.

"Do you know what I touch, here?" she asked. She put both her hands on her left side.

"Yes, ma'am."

"What do I touch?"

"Your heart, ma'am."

"Broken!" She said it as if she were proud of her broken heart. She gave me a strange smile. Then she said, "I am tired. I want some entertainment. Play." I stood there, not knowing what to do. "I have funny ideas sometimes," she said. "And I have this funny idea that I want to see a child at play. Now, play. Play!"

I couldn't move. This strange old woman wanted me to play. How could I? She scared me; the house scared me. It was all too new. I'd never been inside

such a fine place. And I was afraid of doing something wrong.

"What's the matter with you?" Miss Havisham asked. "Why won't you play?"

"I'm sorry," I said. "It's all so new and strange here, and so sad. And I'm afraid of what my sister would do to me, if I did something wrong. I would play if I could, but . . ."

"So new to him," she said, "so old to me. So strange to him, so familiar to me. So sad to both of us! Call Estella."

I didn't know if she was talking to me or not. "Call Estella," she said again. "You can do that. Call Estella. At the door." I did as I was told.

In a few minutes, the beautiful young girl showed up. "Let me see you play cards with this boy," Miss Havisham told her.

"With this boy?" she asked, "Why, he's nothing but a common lower-class boy!"

"Well," Miss Havisham said, "you can break his heart."

"What do you play, boy?" Estella asked, her voice full of scorn.

I knew only one card game. It's called "beggar my neighbor." It's a simple game I had learned from Joe. I told Miss Havisham this. "Then go ahead and play," she said.

We went through only two games. Estella beat me both times without even trying. But it wasn't losing that bothered me so much. It was the way Estella treated me. She made fun of me because I called the knaves in the deck *jacks*. I thought everyone did. It was how I had learned.

"And what rough, ugly hands he has," Estella went on. "And such thick, clumsy shoes."

Every time I made a mistake, and I didn't play well, Estella would insult me again. She laughed at me and called me a stupid lower-class boy. After a time, Miss Havisham said to me, "What do you think of Estella?"

"She is very proud and very pretty," I said.

"She says awful things about you," said the old lady. "What do you say to that?"

"I say she is very insulting. I don't know why she has to treat me like this."

"Anything else?"

"Yes, ma'am. I want to go home."

"Very well," the old lady said. "You will come again, in six days. Estella, give the boy some food, and let him look around the place while he eats. Go, Pip."

I followed Estella downstairs. She led me outside. "You will wait here, boy," she said. She came back with some food and drink. She put it on the ground, as if I were a dog. Then she walked away.

I was so hurt I cried. I kicked my thick shoes against the wall and pulled the hair on my head. This helped me get rid of my bitter feelings. I stopped crying. Finally, I ate the food. I had just finished when Estella came back.

"Why don't you cry?" she asked.

"Because I don't want to."

"You do," she said. "You've been crying until you're half blind. And you're almost crying now." She laughed at me and pushed me outside the gate. I walked the four miles back to my home.

As I walked, I knew I had learned something. I was a common, lower-class boy. My hands were ugly and my shoes were clumsy. I called knaves *jacks*. I think I was the unhappiest child in the world.

4 I Become Joe's Apprentice

When I got back from Miss Havisham's house, both my sister and Mr. Pumblechook wanted to know what happened there. "How did you get on uptown?" he asked.

"Pretty well," I said.

"Pretty well is no answer," said my sister. She hit me on my ears. What could I say? I knew that if I told the truth, they wouldn't believe me. I could hardly believe it myself.

So I lied. I told them that Miss Havisham lived in splendor. I said that she had a fancy coach in her room, that we all ate wonderful food, and that her dogs fought for the scraps. Both my sister and Mr. Pumblechook believed it right away. That's when I knew that neither of them had ever been inside Miss Havisham's house.

It didn't bother me that I was lying to my sister and Mr. Pumblechook. Mostly, I said what I did just to make my sister stop hitting me. But it hurt me to see Joe taking in every word and believing the story. Later on, I went to Joe and told him the truth. He wasn't mad at me. All he did was tell me never to lie again.

But the hurt caused by what Estella had said stayed with me. I made up my mind that no matter what, I would no longer be "common." I still wasn't making much progress in my lessons at school. But there was one student, Biddy, who seemed to be doing very well. Biddy was an orphan, like me. But she had seen much more of the world than I. Perhaps she could help me. I asked Biddy if she would teach me everything she knew, and she agreed to do this. I did my best at my lessons, and I tried as hard as I could not to be common.

Joe would sometimes like to smoke his pipe at a bar in town. Because the place, called the Three Jolly Bargemen, was near my school, I would often meet Joe there, afterward. One day, not long after my visit to Miss Havisham's, I went to the Three Jolly Bargemen to meet Joe.

When I went in, he was sitting near the fire. Mr. Wopsle and a man I'd never seen before were sitting with him. The stranger asked Joe if I were his son. Joe explained how I came to live with him, and that one day I would be his apprentice.

The stranger then bought a drink for Joe and Mr. Wopsle. He ordered rum and water. When the drinks came, Mr. Wopsle and Joe were lost in talk. The stranger stirred his drink. But he didn't use a stick or a spoon. When he saw that the others weren't watching him, he took out a file and stirred his rum and water.

I knew the file right away. It was the one I had stolen from Joe and given to my convict. The way the man looked at me said it all. Plainly, he knew who I was, and he knew my convict. He put the file away and began to talk with Joe and Mr. Wopsle.

Before I left with Joe, the stranger said, "Stop half a minute, Mr. Gargery. I think I've got a bright new shilling in my pocket. If I do, the boy may have it."

He reached into his pocket, and wrapping the coin in a piece of paper, handed it to me. I thanked him, and we left. It wasn't until we got home that I looked at it. Yes, it was a bright new shilling. But the paper it was wrapped in was also money: two one-pound notes. This was a great sum of money in those days.

Of course, I didn't get to touch the money. My sister took it and put it in a teapot she kept over the fireplace. That night, I had bad dreams. I could see the file coming at me through a door. Before I could see who held it, I woke up screaming.

Six days had passed, and I was due to see Miss Havisham and Estella again. Once again, Estella let me in at the gate. This time, we went to a different room in the house. There were three people I'd never seen before. They spoke of things of which I knew nothing. I later found out that they were Miss Havisham's cousins.

They all stood around in this very big room. There was a great table in the room. On it, as a centerpiece, was a black, rotten object. I couldn't say what it was. When Miss Havisham came into the room, she had a fight with her cousins, and they left, angry. I was left alone with her.

"This is my birthday, Pip," she said. "That is why my cousins were here." She pointed to the rotten *thing* in the middle of the table. "Do you know what that is?" she asked.

"No, ma'am."

"It is my wedding cake," she said. "It is rotting away, just as I am. One day, when I die, I will be laid out on the table with it."

Then, she had me play cards with Estella again. Estella was as nasty to me as ever. Finally, it was time for me to leave. I didn't need Estella to show me out. I knew the way now.

As I was getting ready to leave, I came across a pale young gentleman. He was about my age. I didn't know who he was, but he wanted to fight with me. I didn't want to, but he hit me and butted me with his head. I had to fight him then. To my great surprise, I beat him badly.

When I got to the courtyard, Estella was waiting to let me out. Instead of going straight to the gate,

she waved me to a hall. "Come here," she said. "You may kiss me, if you like."

I kissed her on the cheek. But in my heart, I knew that allowing a common lower-class boy to kiss her meant no more to her than giving a dog a bone.

For the next ten months, I visited Miss Havisham once a week. She had gotten a wheelchair, and it was my job to push her around the big old house. Estella was, by turns, rude or pleasant to me. That is, pleasant for Estella.

One day, Miss Havisham asked me about Joe. I told her about my becoming Joe's apprentice one day. She said she wanted to meet Joe, and she had me bring him to the house. My sister had a fit because she wasn't asked, too.

Joe put on his best clothes, and we went to the big house. Joe didn't know what to say to Miss Havisham. Once he saw the strange house and the stranger way Miss Havisham lived, he had even less to say. Miss Havisham did most of the talking.

She asked Joe if I were to become his apprentice. Joe said yes. "Does the boy like the trade?" she asked. I said I did. What happened next was a wonderful surprise. "Pip has earned money, coming here," she said. "Take this, for his learning." And she gave Joe twenty-five pounds!

In those days, it was quite common for a boy to be taken on as an apprentice. His parents had to

pay the man whose trade he would be learning. Of course, I had no money to pay Joe. And he didn't expect any. We both thanked Miss Havisham.

"Good-bye, Pip," said Miss Havisham. "Let them out, Estella."

"Am I to come again?" I asked.

"No," she said. "You belong to Gargery now."

So it was that I became Joe's apprentice. The papers were filed at the town hall. Then, when my sister found out that Miss Havisham had given Joe twenty-five pounds, there was a party. Twenty-five pounds was more than Joe would have made in a year. Of course, at the party, given with the money I had earned, I got little to eat and drink. But my sister and Mr. Pumblechook had a great time.

I went back to Miss Havisham's once after that, to pay her a visit. What I really wanted to do was see Estella. In spite of all she had done to me, I think I loved her. Maybe it was because she was out of reach for a common boy like me.

But I wasn't to see her. I found out that she had been sent to school in France. I decided then that I would work harder at my own schooling. When Estella came back, I would be well schooled. She would see that I was a gentleman, not just a "common lower-class boy."

5 "A Young Man of Great Expectations"

One day, not long after that, I stopped in at the Three Jolly Bargemen on my way home from school. Everyone there was excited. They were talking about the terrible thing that had happened. As I listened, I realized they were talking about Joe's house! I ran home to find that my sister had been badly hurt.

Someone had broken into our house while Joe was out. My sister had been hit on the back of the head. She lay on the floor, nearly dead. No one knew who did it. But next to her was a convict's leg chain.

My sister never completely recovered. She could no longer talk. She couldn't do her housework, either. So it happened that Biddy came to live with us. I was happy about this, even though I felt bad for my sister. If Biddy stayed with us, I could learn more from her. Soon, I was reading and writing well.

One Sunday, Biddy and I took a long walk out on the marshes. I told her I wanted to become a gentleman, and that it was because of Estella. Biddy said, "Pip, if you have to change yourself to win her over, then she is not worth winning over."

I knew Biddy was right, but I couldn't change the way I felt.

And so the years passed. I must say that all my learning didn't make me very happy. The more I learned, the more I realized how "common" I was. I was unhappy with my trade, and I was ashamed of my home.

In my fourth year as Joe's apprentice, something happened that changed my whole life. I was with Joe and Mr. Wopsle, at the Three Jolly Bargemen. Mr. Wopsle was reading from a paper about a murder case. As usual, he was telling anyone who'd listen his ideas about the case.

"You know nothing about it," said a voice, and we all looked around.

A well-dressed man I'd never seen before had spoken. He was a big heavy man, with a red face and a loud voice.

"And I'm sure that *you* do?" said Mr. Wopsle.

"I had better," said the red-faced man. "My name is Jaggers. I am a lawyer in London, and I am pretty well-known. I have worked on more murder cases than you've ever read about."

Mr. Jaggers was so big, and his voice so loud, that even Mr. Wopsle was quiet. "But that is not why I have come here from London," Jaggers went on. "I have come to see a Joe Gargery. Does anyone know where I might find him?"

"Why, that's me, sir," said Joe.

"And you have an apprentice called Pip?"

"I do, sir. This is the lad, right here."

"Then I must speak with both of you privately."

There are a few small private rooms at the Three Jolly Bargemen. We went to one. No sooner were we sitting down when Jaggers took over. As he spoke, my eyes grew bigger and bigger.

"I have come," said Jaggers, "to see Pip off to London. It seems that he is to become a gentleman. A certain person, whose name I can't give, has put aside a great deal of money for the boy. I am to be his guardian, and he is to be well dressed and educated. He is now a young man of great expectations."

I can't tell you how happy this made me. I also knew in my heart the "person" Jaggers couldn't name. It had to be Miss Havisham!

"Now," Jaggers said to Joe, "how much money do you want?"

I knew what Jaggers meant. If I were taken away, Joe would lose his apprentice. He'd have to find another and train him. That would cost him time and money. But Joe, God bless him, asked for nothing. He was the same kind, gentle Joe as ever. He had been better to me than my own sister ever was.

The next few days flew by. I got more new clothes than I knew what to do with. The day before I was to leave for London, I went to see Miss Havisham. I wanted to thank her. But I also knew she wanted her gift to me to stay a secret. So, I said, "I have come into such good fortune since I last saw you, and I am very grateful, Miss Havisham." She was kind, and wished me luck.

Next morning, at five o'clock, dressed in my best clothes, I waited for the coach to London. I'm

ashamed to say that I had told Joe I wanted to walk to the coach alone. Now that I had such fancy clothes, I didn't want to be seen with Joe. So, after a quick breakfast, I had said good-bye to Joe, Biddy, and my sister. If I hadn't rushed off then, I would have burst into tears.

The coach came, and I got inside. As it left the only town I'd ever known, I felt the whole world was spread out before me!

6 *Herbert Pocket*

What can I say about London? It terrified me. Yes, I had read about the great city. Yes, I had seen pictures. But even though you read about an elephant and see pictures of it, it means nothing until you stand next to one.

I found Mr. Jaggers's office. It was on a gloomy street in a rotten section of London. I thought that he should have a nicer, cleaner place. But it seemed to please Jaggers to have his office here. His work was to defend criminals. So he kept his office in a bad part of town, where criminals often lived.

His waiting room was full of people. They all made my convict of so many years ago look good. The clerk showed me in to Jaggers's private office. It was no nicer than the waiting room. Worse, in fact, because of two plaster casts of faces. They were horrible, swollen things. Looking at them could make you sick. They didn't bother Mr. Jaggers, though. He was eating a sandwich.

"Come in, boy," he said in his booming voice. "We must get things in order for you. You need a place to live. You will stay with a young man I know, at Barnard's Inn. His name is Herbert

Pocket." He gave me what seemed to me a great deal of money. "Here is your allowance, boy," he boomed. "You must start living like a gentleman."

He hardly gave me a chance to say anything. Next thing I knew, his clerk, Mr. Wemmick, was walking me to Barnard's Inn. I expected it would be a fancy place. It wasn't. In fact, the outside didn't look as good as Joe's blacksmith shop. I saw a name on one of the mailboxes. It read "H. Pocket." There was a note, too. It said he was out shopping for food and would be back soon. Mr. Wemmick showed me up the stairs to Herbert Pocket's rooms. He left me standing at the door.

I waited there for half an hour. Finally, a young man came up the stairs, bags of food in his arms.

"Mr. Pip?" he said.

"Mr. Pocket?" I said.

"I am sorry to be so late," he apologized.

Then we both stood there and stared at each other. I was amazed. I knew him. He was the pale young gentleman I had fought with at Miss Havisham's, years ago. He knew me right away, too.

"I can't believe it," he told me. "How do you come to be in London?" He opened the door and invited me in.

As I told my story, he asked many questions. To my surprise, he wasn't a bad fellow at all. I liked him a lot. Looking back, I couldn't think why he

had wanted to fight me that day at Miss Havisham's. He was such a nice young man. Once he heard my story, he told me about himself. I also found out what he had been doing at Miss Havisham's on her birthday.

"My father is Miss Havisham's cousin," he told me. "We all had to go to her house on her birthday." And then he told me a strange tale: "Once, Miss Havisham was young and very pretty. Her father was very, very rich. He owned a big brewery. Miss Havisham's mother died when she was just a child. Then Mr. Havisham, my great-uncle, married his cook, in secret.

"They had a son. When the old man died, he left half his money to Miss Havisham and half to his son. The son spent it all, in no time. He also sold his half of the brewery for next to nothing. He sold it to a stranger. He wasn't a *gentleman*, you see."

I nodded. I was beginning to see how important being a gentleman was.

"Anyway," Herbert went on, "once this stranger saw Miss Havisham, he went after her. He said he loved her. But he was after her money and the other half of the brewery. I don't know how much money she gave him. It was a lot, though. My father warned her about him. But Miss Havisham was in love. She and my father had a bad fight. They didn't speak to each other for years after that."

"So she married this man?"

"Use your head, man," said Herbert. "If she'd married, she wouldn't be *Miss* Havisham, would she? Yes, they were supposed to be married. All the plans were made. Guests were invited; a wedding cake was made. They were to be married at nine in the morning. Then, just twenty minutes before nine, a note came. The man had run away. The wedding was off.

"Suddenly, Miss Havisham knew. It was all a trick. Her half-brother and this man were in it together. They got the most money they could, and then they both ran away."

"It must have hurt Miss Havisham something awful," I said.

"Hurt her? You've seen her. She went out of her mind. She never left the house again. She walks around in her wedding dress, after all these years. All the clocks in the house are stopped at twenty to nine."

"But what of Estella?" I asked. "Who is she, then?"

"To tell you the truth, I don't know. I do know that Miss Havisham adopted her. Then again, my father doesn't tell me everything. There must be more to the story, but I don't know it. I do know something else about Estella, though."

"Tell me, please, do," I said.

"You rather like her, don't you?" said Herbert, with a smile. "Well, I wouldn't if I were you. Miss Havisham raised Estella for one reason. To break men's hearts. You see, through Estella, she wants to get even with all men."

Suddenly, it all made sense to me. The clocks stopped at twenty to nine, the rotten wedding cake, Miss Havisham's yellowed wedding dress. And Estella . . . my beloved Estella. But in my heart, I knew Herbert was wrong about her. I loved her, and I hoped that one day she would come to love me, too.

"But enough of this," said Herbert with a grin. "We have to go to dinner at my father's house. He will be your new teacher. He's quite the smartest man in London. There's just one thing he doesn't know."

"What's that?"

"How to make money," laughed Herbert. "He has to rent out rooms in his house. That, plus what he makes at teaching, lets him live. But that's not for me. I'm going into the insurance business."

"Oh, really?" I asked. "Where do you work?" He named one of the big companies. "And do you make a lot of money there?"

"Uh, well, . . . to tell the truth," he said, "I don't make anything. I work there to get experience." His face brightened. "And when I do," he said, "I shall be very rich, indeed."

I didn't say anything. It seemed to me that Herbert didn't know any more than his father about making money. Not if he was working for no pay at all. But why should I hurt his feelings? He was such a nice fellow.

7
My Life in London

Dinner at Mr. Pocket's house was an eye-opener to me. Herbert's father, Matthew, was a lovely, gentle man. And there seemed to be children everywhere. The servants ran the house because Mrs. Pocket couldn't. She was a sweet person but quite unable to do a thing. For all that, Mr. Pocket and Herbert loved her.

After a few hours with Mr. Pocket, I knew Herbert was right. This would be the man to teach me. He seemed to know everything in the world.

Mr. Pocket's house was so large that he was able to rent out some of the rooms. He introduced me to the people who rented rooms there. One was a very nice, handsome fellow named Startop. We got along right away. But the other was a brute named Bentley Drummle. He made Mr. Jaggers seem shy. I have never met a nastier chap. So, you can imagine how surprised I was to find out that Drummle was a "gentleman." In fact, when his father died, Drummle would become a baronet . . . a lord!

I made up my mind to see as little of Drummle as I could. But it was not to be. He, Herbert, Startop, and I were invited to dinner at Mr.

Jaggers's house. Startop, as ever, was polite, and a pleasure to be with. But Drummle! He drank too much and once even insulted Mr. Jaggers. I waited for the explosion. Now, Mr. Jaggers would put this brute in his place.

"Quite the spider, aren't you?" Jaggers said to Drummle. Then he laughed. "Well, I don't fear you, even though you're young and strong," he said. "I want you to meet someone. Molly!"

The cook who had served our dinner came in. She was a big woman, nearly the size of a large man. She came up to Jaggers.

"Yes, sir?"

Jaggers made no reply. He grabbed Molly's hand, and I saw that her wrist was badly scarred. He held it under Drummle's nose. "Do you see this?" he boomed. "This woman's wrists and hands are stronger than those of any man. I defended her for murder, once. Give me no trouble, Spider, or I'll have her break you in two, like a dried stick!" Then he laughed loud and long. "And look at that face. I saved her from being another face in my office."

"Have you seen those faces?" Herbert whispered to me.

"Yes," I said. "They're horrible."

"They are death masks," Herbert said. "Made after the two were hanged for murder. That's why they are so swollen and horrid."

Then dinner was over. Jaggers saw us out and made a great fuss about Drummle. He actually liked the monster. I guessed it was because Drummle was as big a bully as Jaggers himself.

The weeks went by. I soon found myself more and more with Startop and Drummle. They were gentlemen, and so must I be. I also found out that being a gentleman was easy. All one had to do was drink, carry on, go to parties, and spend money. At this last, I found I had a talent.

I bought more clothes. I bought dinner for my new friends. I bought a boat and learned to row on the River Thames, as gentlemen did. In a short time, I was out of cash. But what did it matter? I knew I would be getting more.

Of all the money I spent, there was one thing I did that wasn't selfish. Secretly, I paid a large amount of money to a shipping firm. They agreed to take in my friend Herbert Pocket as a junior partner. The look on his face when he found out was payment enough for me.

Before long, I was deep in debt. Through it all, I dreamed of the lovely Estella. Surely, if she could see me now, she'd know me for a gentleman. What I didn't know was that I was also becoming the worst kind of snob. I wanted to forget the fact that I hadn't always been a gentleman.

One day I received a letter from Biddy, saying that Joe was coming to visit me the next morning.

I thought about all the money I had spent furnishing the rooms. Joe would look so common and out of place here. I wished he were not coming!

Joe came early the next day. I heard his thick boots on the stairs. Then I heard him wiping them on the doormat. I opened the door.

"Joe! How are you?"

"Fine, Pip. And yourself?" said Joe, his face shining with joy. "Why, you're a real gentleman now!"

I asked Joe about my sister and Biddy.

"Your sister is no worse," said Joe. "Biddy is well. She's been a real blessing in the house. She's even promised to teach me to read and write."

I invited Joe to sit down and have breakfast with me. As we talked, I noticed that Joe was becoming more and more uneasy. Finally he said, "Pip, I came here to bring you a message from Miss Havisham."

"Yes, Joe," I cried eagerly.

"Miss Havisham said, 'Tell Pip that Estella is back, and that she'll be glad to see him.' "

My heart skipped a beat, and my face grew red.

"And now I'll be going," said Joe. "I've said what I had to say. I must be going home."

"Won't you stay for dinner, Joe?"

"No, Pip."

We looked at each other.

"Pip, you know that this is no place for me. I'm a blacksmith. My place is the forge. I don't belong here. I don't feel myself here. Good-bye, Pip! May God bless you, dear old Pip!"

With that, Joe left. Dear, good, honest Joe!

My thoughts returned to Miss Havisham's message. Estella was back again! I must see her. I booked a seat on the next day's coach. Dressed in my finest clothes, I rode back to my hometown with my heart in my throat. Estella, at last!

When I got there, it was late in the evening. I knew I should stay at the forge with Joe. But I didn't. Instead, I stayed at an inn called the Blue Boar. It was much nicer than the Three Jolly Bargemen. I'm ashamed to say that the next day I didn't go to see Joe or Biddy. I went straight to Miss Havisham's.

I hardly knew Estella. She had been beautiful as a child. But now, she was by far the loveliest thing I'd ever seen. A light seemed to surround her, brightening the gloom of Miss Havisham's room.

"Is she changed, Pip?" Miss Havisham asked.

"Beyond my dreams," I said.

"Is he changed, Estella?" asked Miss Havisham.

"Yes," she replied. "He is much less coarse and common."

Miss Havisham got to her feet. She put Estella's arms around my neck. "Love her, Pip," the old woman said. "Love her with all your heart. Now, you two, go walk in the garden. Be together in the light. I must stay forever in darkness."

We walked together, and for a second, I felt like that little boy again. Estella was so lovely. "You mustn't love me, Pip," she said. "No matter what Miss Havisham says."

"It's too late," I said.

"You must know," Estella said, "that I have no heart at all. No love to give anyone. It's how I was raised. But you may see me from time to time. I will be living near London, in Richmond."

My heart leaped. My beloved would be near. I could call on her—see her. In time, I would prove her words wrong. She would come to love me. I would make it happen! I was in heaven all the way back to London. It *did* bother me a bit that I didn't go to see Joe and Biddy. But after all, they were no longer of *my* class. I sent Joe a fine present and forgot about it.

And so it went. My days were mostly taken up with lessons with Mr. Pocket and visits with Estella. Evenings, I would go out drinking and gambling with the gentle Startop and the hateful Drummle. One night, when we'd all had a bit too much to drink, Drummle got to his feet and raised a glass.

"To the most beautiful woman in London," he said, "Miss Estella Havisham!"

"Who are you to speak her name?" I cried.

"Who are you to even know her?" sneered Drummle. "You may have fine clothes and some learning. But under it all, you are common. I am to be a baronet."

"I don't care. You will not mention her name in a bar," I cried angrily.

"I will mention her name wherever and whenever I choose," said Drummle. "She is to be my wife!"

"Is this true?" I demanded.

"I wouldn't bother to lie to such as you," said Drummle. "I know all about you, Pip. Estella and I have laughed many times about you."

I ran from the bar. I was half drunk, and tears blinded me.

How could she have done this? Then I remembered Herbert's words about how Miss Havisham had raised Estella. Oh, God, it was all true!

Somehow, I got to my rooms. Not since the day Estella had made me cry, was I so hurt. I thought my world had ended. Nothing worse could ever befall me. How wrong I was!

8 "My" Convict Returns

Shortly after the fight with Drummle, I got another letter from Biddy. My sister had died. Just before she passed on, she spoke two words: "Joe," and then, "Pip." I went to the funeral, but somehow, that body in the coffin wasn't Mrs. Joe Gargery to me. Not the ever-loud, red-faced woman who used the Tickler on me.

I'm ashamed to say that I didn't stay long. I didn't want to be seen too much with Joe and Biddy, with their working clothes and ways. I did pay a visit to Miss Havisham. And naturally, she

spoke of Estella. The old lady was upset. She felt her death was near, and she wanted someone—*anyone*—to love her. She wanted this from Estella. But she had raised Estella too well. True to her words to me, Estella could love no one. Not even Miss Havisham. I left the old lady to her bitter memories and returned to London.

As I went up the stairs to my rooms, I thought I saw a man in the shadows. I got only a quick look. But there was something familiar about him. Putting it from my mind, I entered my rooms.

Later that evening, as I was about to go to bed, I heard footsteps on the stairs. Somebody was trying to find his way upstairs in the dark.

I took my lamp and went to the top of the stairs.

"Who is it?" I shouted. "Which floor do you want?"

"The top floor. I'm looking for Mr. Pip," a voice replied. The man came slowly forward into the light of the lamp.

"Who are you, sir?" I said.

He was old, I'd say in his sixties, with gray hair. But he seemed strong, and his voice was clear when he said to me, "Don't you know me, Pip?"

"I'm afraid I do not, sir. What is your business?" I asked him.

"If you let me come in, I'll explain everything," he said.

I didn't care to have a visitor so late at night, but I showed him into my rooms. He looked around and seemed pleased by what he saw. Then he walked over to a chair and sat down.

"Maybe you'll remember me now," the old man said. He took a handkerchief from his coat pocket and tied it around his head. Then he took a file from his jacket and made motions as if he were freezing.

"The convict!" I cried.

"Just so," said the old man, with a smile. "And I never forgot how you helped me that Christmas Eve, lad. That's why I have sent you money."

"Oh, yes," I said. "The shilling wrapped in two pounds." I reached inside my coat and took out two one-pound notes. "Here," I said. "And thank you for your kindness."

The old man laughed and waved away the money I offered. "I have no need for it," he said. "I am quite rich." He took out a wallet and showed me. He must have had thousands of pounds! Had he stolen it? "You see," he went on, "after I served some time in the prison ship, I was given a second chance. I could go to Australia as a free man. But I could never return to England again. It would mean death."

I nodded. I knew from Mr. Jaggers that the prisons in England were so crowded, this was often done. In fact, prison boats were used because the jails were so crowded. "But why have you come back?" I asked the old man.

"Why, to see you, Pip," said the man with a fond smile. "Even if it costs me my life, it will have been well worth coming back to England. And haven't you become a fine gentleman?"

"I suppose so, er . . . " What could I call him? One doesn't call a convict by name, does he?

"Magwitch," said the man. "Abel Magwitch. Ah, Pip, it makes me so happy to see you."

I didn't understand. This rough, terrible man was upsetting me. He didn't want the two pounds. He just wanted to see me. But why? I asked him, and he made this reply:

"I never forgot that night, Pip. When I met you, I was trying to see my own child. She was a little girl. I was told that she lived near your town. I didn't even know if she was still alive. I'd never seen her. And I couldn't have cared less for her mother. The girl was, I might say, an accident of birth.

"Then, when I met you in the marshes, you were so brave and true. . . . Well, I began to think of you as my son, all those years in prison."

I was horrified. This rough criminal thought of me, Pip the gentleman, as his son? What an awful idea. But I said nothing. In truth, old as he was, he was still a frightening fellow. I tried to change the subject.

"Tell me," I said, "what was it that put you in jail to begin with?"

"Ah, that's a tale," said Magwitch. "It began near to where I met you. Me and this chap Compeyson were part of a shady deal. He found this rich woman, who owned a brewery. Her own brother put us on to her. Compeyson told the woman he loved her. That he would marry her. She gave him lots of money. Then, when we had enough, away we ran—on the very day Compeyson was to have married. Ahh, he was a cold chap, that Compeyson.

"And the airs he put on! As if he were a fine gentleman . . . excuse me, like yourself, Pip . . . but he was a crook, through and through."

"What happened?" I asked. Suddenly, I was very interested.

"We were caught," Magwitch said. "I got fourteen years, because I didn't talk or act fancy. But Compeyson, that snake, got only seven. His good manners and fancy talk fooled the judge. But not me. I would have killed him, if I could. In fact, I tried."

"The other convict!" I cried. "The one you were fighting with when they found you!"

"Aye, and I would have killed him then. But I thought: What's worse? A clean death, or prison? I know prison's worse. I had decided to bring him back, when we were found. May he rot in hell!" The old man's face softened as he looked at me. "But that's behind me now," he said. "And I've come to see you."

"Well, now that you have . . . ," I began.

"And I have come to give you this," he finished. He again took out the thick wallet. "You are twenty-one now."

"Yes," I said. "But I don't need money from you. Mr. Jaggers has said that soon I will have plenty."

"Ah, has he?" smiled the convict. "And what else did he say of the money you've had all these years?"

"I never knew where it came from," I admitted. "Mr. Jaggers said that once I was twenty-one years old, I'd be told." I saw no reason to tell him of Miss Havisham's kindness to me. Doubly so, because it was Magwitch who helped to break her heart.

"And so you shall be told," said Magwitch, smiling. "It was me that did it, Pip. I've been sending the money to you all these years. And I have come all this way . . . at risk of my life . . . to give the rest of your fortune to you!"

He again held out the money. I nearly fell to the floor. It wasn't Miss Havisham who helped me. I, the fine gentleman, was in the debt of a convict! I had dreamed that Estella might break off with Drummle and that she would see I was a true gentleman. What a joke. This dreadful creature was my "father"! He was the source of my "great expectations." My world was falling down around my ears.

Worst of all, I thought of how I had treated Joe and Biddy. They were "low class" to me then. Little

did I know that good, kind, gentle Joe was far
above me. And I had treated him like dirt. It made
my face turn red as I thought of it. And here was
this *person*, acting as if I were his "son." I sighed
deeply. Well, if I were a convict's adopted son, so
be it.

"You took a terrible chance coming here," I told Magwitch.

"It was long ago that I went to Australia. Nobody in London is interested in me anymore, except my lawyer, Mr. Jaggers. Even if he knew I were here, he'd never tell. I trust Jaggers. It was he that found a good home for my daughter."

My heart jumped into my throat. Nobody who'd be interested in Magwitch? Suddenly, I knew who the man in the shadows was. "You must get out of England right away," I said to Magwitch. "You are in danger."

"From who?" said Magwitch. "I told you no one remembers."

"There is one man," I said. "Compeyson. I saw him hanging around outside, when I came in."

"Then quickly," Magwitch said, "take this money. I must go."

The shame of how I'd acted over the years hit me. I may have been a snob and a fool. But for what he was, Abel Magwitch had done well by me. "No," I said. "I can't take your money. You've done enough for me.

"But I will get you safely out of the country," I said. "I will hide you until I can buy a ticket on a ship to Australia. I have a boat. . . . After it's dark, I will row you out to the ship. No one will see."

"Ah, Pip," Magwitch said. "You're as true a lad as ever."

I smiled and took his hand. I said nothing. I was still filled with horror at this man. In my way, I was a victim of how I was taught, same as Estella. She couldn't love anyone. And I had been taught to despise criminals. But no thought of that. There was work to do!

9

On the River Thames

I left my rooms and went to the steamship office. I got a ticket for Magwitch, in the name of Provis. As I moved through the streets of London, I had the feeling I was being followed. I looked around

every so often. But my schooling as a fine gentleman hadn't prepared me for this. Criminals can tell if they are being followed. Gentlemen don't know.

Herbert agreed to help me row Magwitch out to his ship. The three of us waited until it was quite late. Then, we sneaked out of our rooms and headed for the river, where my boat was ready. Just as we were about to push off, a voice called out, "Stop, in the name of the Crown!"

I looked up and saw police running toward us. And with them was Compeyson. I *had* been followed! "Quickly!" I shouted at Magwitch. "Cast off!" He untied the rope that held my boat to the dock. I began to row, as hard as I could. Maybe in the darkness, we could still get to the ship that waited.

But soon, there were other boats following us. They had lights. The river was alive with police. I rowed harder. Then a boat pulled up next to us. "It's him!" cried Magwitch. "It's Compeyson!" Magwitch stood up in the boat. Leaning over the side, he grabbed Compeyson by the collar.

Suddenly, Herbert cried out, "Look out, Pip!" But it was too late. A huge oceangoing steamer was coming right at us! I felt a terrible *crunch*. Then I was drifting down, under the black water of the Thames.

I awoke in my own rooms. Standing at the foot of my bed was Mr. Jaggers. As I opened my eyes,

he smiled at me. "Back to life, eh, Pip?" he boomed. "We were worried for a while."

"Magwitch?" I asked, weakly.

"Dead," said Jaggers. "And a sorry end it was, poor devil. But better than the hangman's rope. It would have been that, had he lived. At least he took Compeyson with him."

"He could have been safe in Australia," I said. "But he came back to see me. To give me my fortune."

"That, and some other business," said Jaggers.

"What other could it be?" I asked.

"I have the idea he wanted to see his daughter. He never spoke with me, though. God knows I wouldn't have told him where she is."

"Then his daughter is alive?" I asked.

"Very much so," said Jaggers. "You recall my cook, Molly?"

"Yes, sir."

"That was Magwitch's wife. When she went on trial for murder, the daughter fell into my care. She was such a lovely child, I couldn't leave her with a monster like her mother. What chance would she have in life? I found a good home for her.

"When I got her mother off, I told her what I'd done. The woman was grateful to me. So much so, that she remains my servant to this day. She never takes money from me, either."

"Magwitch helped me get on in life," I sighed. "If I can, I will help his daughter."

"Help yourself, lad," said Jaggers. "With Magwitch gone, so is your money. The police got the fifty thousand pounds he had for you. You owe everyone. As you have no money, you'll be put in debtor's prison. Get back your health, boy, and think of your future. If you have one."

Jaggers started to go. Weakly, I called to him from my bed. He stopped in the doorway. "Please, sir," I asked. "If I do get out of this, I must help Magwitch's daughter. Where is she? What is her name?"

Jaggers laughed. "She doesn't need your help, Pip. I suppose there's no harm in telling you now. You'll never see her again."

"Again? I don't understand."

"You grew up playing with her, boy. Magwitch's daughter is Estella Havisham."

The room spun around. Blackness came over me. I knew no more of the world for the next four weeks. I recall being sick, alone. I dimly recall the police. They had come to take me to debtor's prison, but I was too ill to be moved.

The next time I awoke, Joe Gargery was by my side. He told me that Herbert had gone to the Far East on a business trip. Before leaving, he had gotten word to Joe about what had happened to me. Little by little, I got back my health. Soon I was up and walking around my rooms. This pleased Joe. Then one day, not long after that, he said, "Well, Pip, I must be going. There's no one tending my shop. And I have Biddy to think of." He smiled shyly. "We're to be married, Pip."

"That's wonderful," I said. "I must come to the wedding."

"No need, Pip. I had to put it off, until you were well. But as soon as I return, we'll be wed. You get well, boy. That's the most important thing."

I thanked Joe with all my heart. I didn't insist on coming with him. I would have, but I just remembered I was a wanted man. As soon as I was well, they would come for me. Debtors' prison was now my future. I didn't say a word to Joe about it, though.

It wasn't until days after Joe left that I found it—a simple note from Joe. He had taken his life's savings and paid my debts! Shame swept over me. He had nursed me, paid my debts, and left. How could I ever face him again? What a wonderful man he was.

And my own life was almost a joke. I had put on airs, acting as if I were better than most people. But my money came from Magwitch, the convict. My great love, Estella, for whom I had longed— made myself a gentleman for—was the daughter of a convict. And now, she was the wife of a lord!

10 *Eleven Years Later*

It was Herbert Pocket who saved what was left of my life. He was doing well in the shipping business. He got me a job in his company. He knew nothing about how I'd helped him, when I had money. He did it because he was a true friend.

I went to the Far East to work with Herbert. Over the years, I grew wealthy through my own efforts. I was now a third partner in Herbert's firm. Yet, I could never bring myself to go back to England. Each time I thought of Joe and Biddy, I was ashamed. And knowing Estella was married to Drummle was too much for me. It wasn't until eleven long years later that I got off the coach in my old hometown.

It hadn't changed much. I walked out to the churchyard, to look at my parents' gravestones. I almost didn't find them. They had fallen down, and the weeds had grown over them. I stood there, thinking of all that had begun at this very place, nearly twenty-five years ago. Then, I turned and walked toward Joe's house.

He was working at the forge when I got there. Bless him, Joe greeted me warmly. Joe had done well. In fact, when I tried to repay him for my old debts, he waved a hand. "No need, Pip," he said. "It's enough to see you again. So grown-up and fine as ever. Biddy and I are proud of you. But come inside. I've something to show you."

We went in, and Biddy greeted me with smiles and kisses. She and Joe now had two children: a boy and a girl. Biddy held up the young lad. "A fine boy," I said. "What's his name?"

Biddy gave me the same girlish smile I recalled so well. "We have named him Pip," she said. "But do sit down, and have a bit to eat."

At the table, Joe and Biddy told me of the events of the past eleven years. Miss Havisham had died, unloved. But she left almost everything to the cold, ungrateful Estella. A small amount had gone to Herbert Pocket.

"And what of Estella, herself?" I asked. "What-ever became of her?"

"A sad story, Pip," Joe said. "Her fine husband used her badly, the brute. He ran around with other women, drank, and gambled. Then he made her shame public. He spent her money, and then he died in an accident . . . abusing a horse, he was. The animal kicked him to death. All she has left is the big old house. And that won't be for long. It's to be sold for his bad debts."

"When?" I asked. "And where is Estella?"

"The house goes within the week. As to Miss Estella, she is at the house. She has nowhere else to go." Suddenly, I was on my feet and out the door. It was a long way to the old house, but my feet flew.

The house, untended since Miss Havisham's death, was in bad shape. I found Estella walking in the garden . . . that same garden we walked in, so long ago. But the garden was completely over-grown with weeds. Estella's back was to me as I entered the garden gate. I called her name, and she turned.

"Can it be . . . ?" she asked.

"Yes, Estella, it's Pip."

"Oh, Pip . . . after all these years. So much has happened. . . ."

"Yes," I said gently, "I have been told. "

"I'm so changed, I'm surprised you knew me."

It was true she had changed. The fresh beauty of youth was gone. But something had taken its place. There was now a softness in her eyes I'd never seen before. As she took my hand, I felt a difference. The once proud and cold Estella had become a warm person. "To me, you are as lovely as ever," I told her.

"Do you remember this place?" she asked. "The place we first met?"

"Indeed, I do," I said. "As I remember the day you first let me kiss you."

"So long ago! I let you kiss me because you beat my cousin."

"Herbert and I have become the best of friends," I said.

"Do you still live abroad?" she asked.

"Yes, I do. I have come back for a visit."

"Are you doing well?"

"I work hard," I said. "Therefore, I do well."

"I have often thought of you," Estella said.

"Have you?"

"Very often, lately. I threw away your love, Pip. Back then, I didn't realize what it was worth. But you do have a place in my heart."

"You have *always* had a place in mine, Estella."

We fell silent for a time; then she spoke.

"How hateful I was," she said. "How cruelly I used you. Oh, Pip. I have found I have a heart. I know, for it has been broken. I can never undo

the hurt I brought to you. I can only hope that we may be friends. If you can forgive me." She held out her hand.

"We *are* friends," I said.

I took her hand in mine, and we went out of the ruined garden. The evening mists were rising in the broad, peaceful twilight. I knew, at that moment, we would never part again.